Challenge Accepted!
A Simple Strategy for Living Life on Purpose

JONATHAN,

Thank you for joining my journey & helping me find my purpose.

Praise for *Challenge Accepted!*

"If pursuing a life of mediocrity & unfulfilled purpose is your goal, then you should avoid this book at all costs!"

— Jared Easley
Co-Founder of the Podcast Movement
StarvetheDoubts.com
Coral Springs, FL

"Motivating, intentional, and procrastination-free, *Challenge Accepted!* delivers a step-by-step, full-of-results method to kick-start adventure, inspire a story, and achieve a goal. Woosley's fresh perspective on the hackneyed bucket list is long overdue."

— Shayla Eaton
Curiouser Editing, CuriouserEditing.com
Yukon, OK

"In a book that's both informative and entertaining, James encourages us to dust off our dreams and ambitions and awaken to our own lives. Offering a solid plan of action with practical steps to get there, one thing's for sure: if you're ready to break out of the mundane and 'enter the arena' of your life, *Challenge Accepted!* is a must-read."

— Beth Underwood
Author and Military Writer
BethWrightUnderwood.com
Lexington, KY

"I came into the game of living intentionally much later than James. I was well into my 40's at that time and would have loved having this book to help me make my goals and challenges consciously. James has taken his talents for simple, strategic business planning and created a fun way to pursue the adventures we dream about but often set aside.

This book is a way that you can become *'engaged in work you enjoy on the journey to the goal you've established.'* Thank you, James, for accepting the challenge and making the world a bit better because of it."

— Jill Davis
JillDavisCoaching.com
Colorado Springs, CO

"Life has many obstacles and challenges, so why not create our own? We can take our lives and live with passion, live with intention, and live with the spirit of GOD leading our hearts to help others.

My challenge began the day I started writing down my desires, stepped back, and saw the paper with my handwriting on it. I had a plan! I had GOALS! I had DREAMS! This is something that I had lost in all the years of school, being a wife and mother, and having a career. Somewhere, somehow, I lost myself.

James has a purpose and is helping others find their way. He has encouraged me to be more than I am and the sky is the limit! Read this book and begin your journey!"

—Toni Amequito
Katy, TX

"Let me add my huge thumbs up to *Challenge Accepted!* I love the wisdom it shows us in how to be intentional as well as how to inject some adventure into our lives. It's not only understandable, but the application behind it is solid! If you're stuck or longing for a change, this may just be the easiest and most fun way to find your path forward and get moving again."

—Robert de Brus
RobertdeBrus.com
Atlanta, GA

"Wow! James has done it again. *Challenge Accepted!* shows us by example, how to live more intentionally while enjoying the present in our journey. James is a master at sharing his story while guiding us to shape ours. Accept the challenge and come alive."

—Mark Ross
Executive, City of Houston
Parks and Recreation Dept.
Houston, TX

"This book is a gift of goal accomplishing from start to finish. James Woosley reminds us to 'Enjoy the Journey' of life and the power of acknowledging when we start and when we finish in order to makes our mission measurable.

It is a must-read for all conscious creators, mentors, and teachers who have a desire to expand their sphere of influence and enhance the life they live."

—Tracy J. Roberts
Abundant Life Ministries, Intl.
Santaquin, UT

"*Challenge Accepted!* is a wonderful, simple, and smart book that is about far more than setting goals. James lays out a path for living an energized life where the journey is full of unexpected rewards. He demystifies the how-to and makes our seemingly impossible dreams very achievable."

— **Jeff Beaudin**
JeffBeaudin.com
Franklin, TN

"This book made me laugh, get teary, but most importantly, it made me think. In my work, I've made it a point to tell others the importance of being intentional and living the life they imagined. But was I really doing the same?

Because of James and his book, I have started my own challenge—60 Before 60. Sixty is a huge number for me, but focusing on completing sixty things that will be significant to my life and the lives of those around me is exciting! Learn to say YES to the opportunities; that's what living is all about!"

— **Missy Day**
Passion 4 Success, Passion4Success.net
Henderson, NV

"James Woosley's *Challenged Accepted!* is a must read if you are looking for practical advice, wisdom, and experience in strategies for obtaining goal success. Join me in accepting the challenge!"

— **Bea Smith**
Elgin, IL

"*Challenge Accepted!* gives you ideas for enjoying your goals along the way. The examples James added of his goals and follow up with the results and how he adjusted them along the way were helpful."

— **Eva P. Scott**
Owner of Scott Secretarial
Author of *Joy & Trouble Joined at the Hip*
Greensboro, NC

"If you want to start living a life of purpose then please take time to read *Challenge Accepted!* It is what you need to jumpstart your SUCCESS. But James doesn't want you to just read this book; he encourages you to APPLY it, and he gives you action steps and a very simple process to begin today."

— **Nicholas Theoharis**
Lake Geneva, WI

"James begins *Challenge Accepted!* by saying 'My ultimate challenge was about showing [my children] how to live an intentional life by living one myself.' Later on, he shares 'I want the scars and the stories that come from real life and real adventure.' In between he inspires us to not only accept the challenge to live on purpose, but also the recipe to get it done!

GREAT book. Powerful, clear, and quick read. Loved it."

— **Chuck Bowen**
CEO, Mission Mercantile
San Antonio, TX

"Tired of living the 'Accidental Life' and want to break free? Take action and get engaged in the *Challenge Accepted!* movement! James excels at laying out a practical approach that can help you successfully move toward a more intentional life. Go from amateur to professional with his practical strategies and insights to create your plan to seize control!"

— **Greg Vance**
Chief Purpose Officer,
CareerMeetsPurpose.com
Carmel, IN

"*Challenge Accepted!* is wonderfully and simply written, woven with humor, experience, and insight, to address and distill the most complicated of roadblocks to a meaningful and productive life. This book will help you stitch together the fabric of your own story with intention and color, and lends credence to 'If you fail to plan, you plan to fail'."

— **Travis D. Fuhlendorf, PMP**
Systems Planning & Analysis, Inc.
Folkston, GA

"Who doesn't need challenged every once in a while to spread their wings or push out of their comfort zone, if nothing more than to prove to yourself that you can? Whether you are ready to take on a big challenge or just take a baby step, James Woosley's *Challenge Accepted!* is a must-read. James mixes his strategic knowledge with his flair for simplicity, to create a plan anyone can follow to find success."

— **Diana Bader**
Fresh Canvas, LLC
FreshCanvasCoaching.com
Atlanta, GA

"Become a legend and have a story to tell! *Challenge Accepted!* shows how to create a story worth telling by equipping you to live a remarkable life. Personal stories that inspire, tips on how to get started and follow through to completion—everything you need to make your dry-bone ideas live—it's all here. This is your life. *Challenge Accepted!* will help you live it full out."

— **Melodie Kenniebrew**
MelodieK.com
Las Cruces, NM

"James book inspired me to start my own challenge to complete three major goals. Completing these goals will significantly change my life and the lives of those connected me. James, thanks for inspiring me to drop the excuses and go after my dreams. That's what living is all about!"

— **Bernard K. Haynes**
LeadToImpact.com
Winston, GA

"Inspired by watching James' journey with his own challenge, I started one on my own but had no framework to go by and struggled through the whole thing. I ended it feeling like it was too much work to ever do again. If I had read *Challenge Accepted!*, I would have known the steps I needed to take which would have led to a much better experience.

Even though I have a love-hate (well, mostly hate) relationship with structure and processes in my life, James has made *Challenge Accepted!* just structured enough with five simple steps that allow me to start on a solid foundation, yet provides for flexibility and adaptation to suit my personal style—big win for me! With this book in hand, I am excitedly planning my next challenge, knowing I now have what I need to make it an unforgettable adventure!"

— **Amber Hendrickson**
CraftYourCompass.com
Colorado Springs, CO

"What a great book! Tightly written, laser-focused. A quick read, but don't read it quickly! Read it deliberately. Then apply it deliberately. Woosley does an excellent job integrating his story into the 'how to' discussion—leaving you encouraged as well as informed. A combination of, 'now I know what to do' and, 'hey, I can do this, too!'"

— **Randy Little, Ph.D.**
AgCollegeAdvocate.com
Starkville, MS (Hail State!)

Purpose | Intensity | Adventure

JAMES WOOSLEY

FOREWORD BY JODY BERKEY

FREE AGENT PRESS

SATSUMA, ALABAMA

Challenge Accepted!:
A Simple Strategy for Living Life on Purpose

© 2015 by James Woosley
Published by Free Agent Press, FreeAgentPress.com
Satsuma, Alabama 36572
VID: 20150513

While the author has made every effort to provide accurate Internet addresses throughout the text, neither the publisher nor the author assumes any responsibility for errors, or for changes that occur after publication. Further, the author and publisher do not have any control over and do not assume any responsibility for third-party websites or their content.

ISBN-13: 978-0692445921
ISBN-10: 0692445927
Library of Congress Control Number: 2015907376

Edited by Jennifer Harshman, HarshmanServices.com
Cover Photo by David Mark
⑩ Logo by George Amequito
Layout & Cover Design by James Woosley

This book is dedicated to my family:

My wife, Heather,
and our children, Anna and Ian.

My parents, Barry and Elaine Woosley.

My in-laws, David and Susan Hollingsworth,
and Heather's brother, Michael.

My sister, Pamela Sandvig, and her husband,
Kyle; and my brother, John Woosley, and his
wife Brandi.

My grandparents, James and Marjorie Greer,
and Opal and Faustine Woosley.

No challenge is worth accepting if it fails to
include, honor, and support you.

TABLE OF CONTENTS

FOREWORD

I think my mind is pretty typical: a flurry of potentially great ideas, scattered random thoughts, and a lot of good-but-often-unfulfilled intentions. Comparing my traditional thought process to a bag of popcorn in a microwave is probably a pretty accurate analogy. Pop, pop, pop...some kernels undercooked, some burnt. Tastes good when fresh, but pretty unimpressive if allowed to go stale.

James's mind is different. It's magical. To me, through my outside perspective, it operates like a flawlessly executed laser show: organized, in sync, and awe-inspiring—especially when paired with a great soundtrack.

When I get a good idea, I try to think and organize like James. Know what? It typically works. Case in point: 90 Rev's (our endurance training company) 13-in-13 Challenge. In late 2012, I decided I wanted to run my first half marathon in 2013—my first endurance event ever. James was doing his well-organized, strategically-planned 40 Before 40 Challenge.

I knew I needed to be strategic and consistent throughout my thirteen weeks of training to be successful. I also knew group accountability works well for me. With my coach's help (Coach Steve:

certified triathlon coach, tough guy, and also my husband), we created a training program and invited other newbie runners from across the country to train together and hold each other accountable.

The experience turned out to be more than I could have ever expected. From the relationships and bonds of friendship that were formed within our group over those thirteen weeks, to the unforgettable feeling of running across the finish line hand-in-hand with Steve, it was an amazing experience. It was all the more amazing that James believed in the dream. He trained in our group. He even flew from Alabama to Virginia to run with us.

It happened because of strategic planning. It happened because I set a goal. I created the conditions to fuel the passion and ideas. I surrounded myself with amazing and encouraging people. I thought about and executed what I thought James would do.

Steve and I are at the beginning of 2015 running a different type of race. We've been working on re-launching 90 Rev with triathlon training software that Steve has been painstakingly developing in his spare time for years.

Since we met James on a cruise ship during Dan Miller's first 48 Days Cruise, he's been a big part of our lives. He's been a longtime supporter, Mastermind partner, and most importantly, a friend. He's encouraged and inspired us. He's challenged and reshaped us. He helped fuel our passion to live more intentionally.

When James issues a challenge and offers to be part of your journey, it would be wise to accept the challenge. We are better people for having done so. You will be, too.

Challenge Accepted!

— Jody Berkey
Friend and #1 Fan
January 2015

INTRODUCTION

This is a book designed to inspire. But what exactly is inspiration?

For me, inspiration elicits action based on information and/or emotion. If reading this book elicits a warm feeling, but no action takes place, then I have failed.

This book is about being intentional. And it's the story of the most intentional year of my life (so far).

I hope that in reading the book, you'll be inspired to create your own challenge and start living life on purpose. Use the blank pages at the back of the book to capture your notes and ideas as you read.

Know that this book isn't about a Bucket List or New Year's Resolutions. It's about saying yes to opportunities, whether they whisper or shout from inside your soul. If that isn't enough, feel free to invent some new opportunities along the way. Live a life worth living.

This is my challenge to you: Read the book and start a challenge of your own. Follow the steps in chapter two and do what scares you, what excites you, what you procrastinate on, and what you've always dreamed of.

Conquer your Kryptonite! It's time to go!

CHAPTER ONE:
Ending the Accidental Life

◆

*In the end, it's not the years in your life that count.
It's the life in your years.*

— **Abraham Lincoln**

Turning Forty

On January 8th of 2013, I turned thirty-nine years old, and it wasn't just my thirty-ninth birthday—it was the beginning of my fortieth year on Earth. I wanted to do something to make it meaningful.

Turning forty is a milestone birthday and it isn't easy for most people. It wasn't for me. I've always felt older than my peers. Maybe I have an old soul or something.

I joked that I was forty when I was born, so when I turned forty, I could finally act my age. Yet terms like "middle-aged" and "mid-life" started popping up. Those can be hard to swallow.

Let me share some family history to add a bit of perspective on what I was going through. My father was only twenty years and fifteen days old the day I was born. And as a kid, your father always seems old! I remember my tenth birthday (I got a wallet without any money in it). My father had just turned thirty . . . he was ancient!

The kicker is that my father retired from the United States Air Force after twenty-two years of service at the age of thirty-nine. I was nineteen. I remember speaking at his retirement dinner[1]. I was only nineteen!

---

[1] The poem I wrote for my father is in the epilogue.

Fast-forward twenty years and I'm the one who's thirty-nine. I spent five years in the Air Force myself, but at thirty-nine, couldn't imagine the concept of retirement (neither could my father as he embarked on new careers himself).

I thought of my father's accomplishments—he was a Chief Master Sergeant, the highest enlisted rank in the service—and now at thirty-nine myself, I was just a consultant for a defense company and trying to get a coaching business off the ground. It didn't compare well, but it was a mistake to make a comparison in the first place.

Those kinds of comparisons either artificially inflate our egos or open a pit of ill feelings and push us in. My life has been immensely different from his life, and both have been more than good enough.

Of course, that's easier to say while I sit here writing this at forty-one, having survived my fortieth year!

Being Intentional

My issues with turning forty were not logical. They were purely emotional and I was only focusing on the negative emotions.

I needed to change my perspective. I needed to find a way to celebrate my fortieth birthday and enjoy it.

I wanted this to be a good thing and an exciting thing. I needed to start living my life on purpose instead of going through the motions each day. It was time to be intentional. It was time to make things happen and realize some dreams.

Some people get a violent wake up call. They lose a loved one, or face an illness or accident of their own. That didn't happen for me, and I didn't need to wait for it to happen. I simply decided to wake up to the life I was already living.

Setting the Example

Thankfully, I didn't start having kids as young as my parents did. They were great, but there's no way I could have handled having a baby at eighteen or twenty years old!

My wife and I were twenty-six when our daughter Anna was born, and thirty-one when we adopted our son, Ian. They will have a different perspective on age just from that fact alone. And I don't want to pass my insecurities and negative feelings about turning forty on to them.

I had to set an example for them, but it needed to go beyond the number of laps we get to ride the Earth around the sun. My ultimate challenge was about showing them how to live an intentional life by living one myself.

The Birth of an Idea

It took a few weeks after my birthday, but I finally came up with an idea to help me get through this transition: complete forty goals before my fortieth birthday.

But I didn't want this to be a Bucket List (turning forty is hard enough); it was just a list of goals and fun things to do over the next year.

I find Bucket Lists a bit morbid. They focus on completing an amazing list of things before you die. Yuck. I also don't like that Bucket Lists are focused on a finish date that is unknown. At nearly forty, I was hoping my life was not yet half over. Planning goals for the rest of my life gave me no sense of urgency. It's easy to procrastinate when you think you have forty or more years to do something.

Bucket Lists also tend to include grandiose goals. Now I love a big goal and love working hard to make them happen, but if you have 100 things to do before you die and they require you to marry a millionaire or win the lottery to make them happen, you're setting yourself up for disappointment.

And then there's the sense that it's all about checking boxes and getting the t-shirt and it being all about you and your wants. Maybe some people can do the whole Bucket List thing with the right mindset. I'm not one of them.

The Basic Process

The idea of the 40 Before 40 Challenge[2] didn't exist for long before I started putting a plan together. It's how I'm wired and what I do. In the next chapter, I'll go through the step-by-step process in more detail (and full results are in the appendix). Here's an overview to get your brain juices flowing.

For me it started in an Excel spreadsheet (I'm a nerd). I made a list of things I was planning to do for the year, along with things that I wanted to do. It was nothing more than a brainstorming session for dreams and goals.

Some of the items were big, while others were small. Some were complicated and would take all year to complete, while others were simple and I just had to show up on a certain date. Some were free and some would take considerable resources.

Once I had the basic list together, I grouped the goals into categories. I did this because, as I mentioned before, I'm a nerd. I also created categories because it allowed me to see the list at a higher level and determine if it was out of balance. Though it was my list and for me, I wanted to include my family in the process as much as possible.

---

[2] Visit WoosleyCoaching.com/40 to review the original blog post and each of the monthly updates (typos and all).

I then added a layer of accountability by blogging about the challenge and committing to monthly updates on my website.

The Results

It was a very long but very amazing year. I accomplished so much in my personal and professional life, and I have to believe that this challenge played a positive role in my achievements.

By tapping into my desires and intentions, writing down specific goals, publishing them, and doing monthly updates, I was forced to follow through on internal initiatives like never before. It's easy to follow through for someone else (a boss, a spouse, a kid, etc.). Maybe you're like me, and doing things for yourself is more difficult (even if those things involve and benefit others).

You can review the entire list of my goals and how I did in the appendix, but here are some highlights:

- I completed my first 5K and my first half marathon.
- I rode 103 miles on my bike in a single day, raising more than $2,000 for the Juvenile Diabetes Research Foundation (JDRF).
- I published my first book, *Conquer the Entrepreneur's Kryptonite* (ending a three-year process), and produced the Kindle and Audiobook versions.

- I was recognized on the floor of the Alabama Legislature.
- I taught my son to ride a bike and I went on dates with my wife and daughter.

The challenge was by far a success and something I recommend anyone attempt at least once in their lives (though every year, all year may be pushing it).

I also failed a lot! But the failures were rarely complete failures, as almost all of the goals saw intentional action and had benefits even though they were short of success.

It was a remarkable year that I'll always remember because I lived it on purpose.

Lessons Learned at the End

First off, I wouldn't do it as a 40 *Before* 40, but a 40 *At* 40 Challenge. Turning forty can be an emotional milestone (it was for me at times, as silly as it seems). The list ended up prolonging my "issues" about the age change and put pressure on the upcoming birthday thing for an entire year.

I may have been better off ignoring my age and pretending it wasn't going to happen until the last month or so. Still, having birthdays is way better than not having them, so I'm not complaining! Doing 40 At 40 would have been more positive, showing what I am capable of even in my old age (I'm joking, really!).

Secondly, I would have focused more on the family items on the list. It was a good year, but I fell short on a few dates and events and that disappoints me the most. However, even though I didn't check everything off, I was more focused on my family and spending time with them, so the net effect was positive.

Lastly, I would have put more energy into the list at the beginning. I started it later in January, and didn't accomplish much in the first few months. And some of the long-term items—like walking two million steps—could have used a bit more attention when I had a lot of time to build up a reserve instead of overcoming a deficit at the end. I am a procrastinator by nature in most areas of my life. This was a good exercise in being proactive, but I still didn't do it perfectly.

Lessons Learned a Year Later

After a long year, my challenge ended. I celebrated my fortieth birthday and decided to take a break from any kind of organized challenge.

I still built a strategic plan and I updated my tangible calendar (more on that in the next chapter). There were plenty of goals to accomplish, but not an overarching theme.

Looking back a year after I ended my first challenge, I see that I accomplished a lot. But I didn't feel like I was living as intentionally as I was during the challenge. I wasn't as focused and I wasn't as driven. Some of my better habits started to slip, and some disappeared.

It's hard to say exactly how much of this was due to not having a structured challenge to follow and how much was due to a lot of real-life strife and stress, including facing job uncertainty and loss, beginning to work in my business full-time, and coping with several family health challenges.

In the end, 2014 was a good year filled with plenty of hard things. Yet looking back, I believe having a challenge of some kind would have grounded me. It would have connected me to the moment, and while adding a kind of accomplishment stress, it would have helped me manage the stress associated with everyday life. The goals may have needed adjusting, but having them would have made my life better by prompting me to live in the moment.

A year later, I regret not having a challenge of some kind in 2014. And that, as much as anything, is why I'm writing the book now. I need it as much as you probably do.

CHAPTER TWO:
Accept the Challenge

◆

We are at our very best, and we are happiest, when we are fully engaged in work we enjoy on the journey toward the goal we've established for ourselves. It gives meaning to our time off and comfort to our sleep. It makes everything else in life so wonderful, so worthwhile.

— Earl Nightingale

Step One: Define the Purpose and Parameters

What's Your Motivation?

Anybody can pick a number of goals and a deadline and get something out of the process. That may work well if you have a free spirit, but even then I believe there is a higher calling on this kind of challenge.

That doesn't mean you have to aim to save the world or be altruistic. But you need to understand the point of it all.

If your challenge is to have meaning, you have to define what that meaning is. Is it about advancing an agenda, connecting with people, trying new things, getting active and healthy, or something else? For me, 40 Before 40 was about living intentionally and creating something to make me feel better about getting older.

Make it meaningful to you and make it relevant to what you value in life. This isn't someone else's challenge for you...this is you challenging yourself to live on purpose.

When I was engaged in a challenge, I was a better person because I was engaged in life. I wasn't aimless. So even if my purpose was less-than-perfect, it was more than nothing.

Don't overthink this. Just imagine yourself at the end of the process with a feeling of accomplishment, and make sure that your accomplishment is bigger and better than achieving a new high score on Candy Crush or binge-watching a television series on Netflix.

Define Your Timeline — Sprint or Marathon?

I spent almost an entire year pursuing my 40 Before 40 Challenge. The timeline was a natural fit to go with my fortieth birthday. But a year is a long time and there were times when the whole thing became exhausting.

As you consider the length of your challenge, compare it to running. If your challenge is a sprint, the timeframe will be short and intense. Make it count. Sprints are great for training and learning.

A marathon, on the other hand, would require you to pace yourself. If you sprint the first few miles of a running marathon, you risk not finishing (or you're a freak of nature). A marathon challenge simply means that you have a longer period of time, and while you're taking it seriously, it's not as rushed as a short-term challenge.

I highly recommend a shorter timeframe if you haven't done something like this successfully before, or if the thought of a year is simply overwhelming. Make a serious commitment and stick to it no matter how long it is. It is far better to win a two-month challenge than it is to give up after eight successful months in a yearlong challenge.

Whatever the length of your challenge, there are two dates that matter more than any other: the day you start and the day you finish.

Your start date may be today, or it could be a few weeks from now. Just don't put it too far into the future. Make a commitment to your challenge right now.

And don't even think about doing this without an end date. There has to be a finish line to cross. You can start another challenge on the same day you finish the first one, but leaving it open-ended will make this a forever-long challenge that fizzles into nothingness.

Your end date can be tied to the end of the month or year, your birthday, a special anniversary, or a random date just because you need an end date. But if the date has meaning, it becomes a motivator and something extra to celebrate at the end of the challenge.

I have a 45-year-old client and friend who recently decided to do fifty things before his fiftieth birthday. Five years is a long time! That timeline may be needed, depending on the content of your goals. Just go into something like that aware of the need to make incremental progress. It's doubtful you can do five years worth of goals (or living) in the last five months of a five-year challenge.

How Many Goals?

Doing forty goals before my fortieth birthday made picking a number easy. But filling that number with meaningful goals wasn't as easy. Tracking and working on that many goals at once took significant effort.

I came up with my challenge with almost a year to go. That made forty goals reasonable. If the idea had popped into my head in December, forty goals in one month either would have been unrealistic, or it would have required a much simpler and less significant set of goals.

The number of goals is important because it will play a factor in the quality and intensity of your challenge. Doing forty surface goals in a month would be a significant challenge, but realistic. Doing forty life-altering goals in a month would be impractical, if not impossible.

The amount of meaning you want in your challenge should help you determine the right number of goals.

Your number also needs to fit your lifestyle. If you work eighty hours a week, you need the challenge in order to change your life. However, tackling a ton of big goals may overload you instead of helping you (unless, of course, those are work-related goals and you keep working that much).

At this point in the process you don't have to have an exact number. It's great if you do, but you can also determine your number as you document your possible goals in Step Two.

Step Two: Document Your Goals

The Right Tool

If you've read this far, you've probably already been thinking of some possible goals to put in your challenge. They may frighten or excite you, but they've been bubbling up to the surface of your consciousness.

I hope you've captured them at the end of the book or on a scrap of paper or notepad. If not, this is where you pull them out of your mind and into existence.

I've already noted that I love Excel, so a spreadsheet is my tool of choice for this exercise (visit ChallengeAccepted.info for resources and templates). In a spreadsheet it's easy to sort and shuffle and move things around as the ideas flow. But you should do what's most effective for you—a piece of paper, a whiteboard, sticky notes, mind-mapping software or anything else that allows you to capture and share your ideas.

The First Draft

Begin with a free-flowing documentation of any and every idea that you have. Don't judge them; just capture them. Get them out of your head because you'll forget half of them if you aren't careful. Even a bad idea can be the catalyst for a good one; so don't worry about whether any of them are bad just yet.

And don't constrain yourself to a specific number of goals even if you have a number in mind from Step One. I picked forty goals for my challenge, but when I was brainstorming I had a lot that were impractical or meaningless once I reviewed the list. If I had stopped after the first forty ideas I had, I would have missed some great ones and been stuck with some real duds.

After a bit of time, you'll begin to run out of ideas to put on your list. That's when you declare the first draft complete and move on to Step Three.

Step Three: Assessing Your List

Categorize Your List

With your first draft in hand (or on screen), you can begin to group them into categories. Some categories will appear naturally, while you may need a bit of creativity or prodding to find a home for some goals (or you can just create a Miscellaneous category).

Categories are important because they allow you to gain a new perspective that's in between the overarching whole and all of the microscopic details. You're seeing deeper into the overall challenge, but not so deep that the big picture is missed because of the details.

Having categories also allows you to assess how balanced your challenge is. I wanted to include both personal and business goals in my challenge, but I didn't want to exclude my family (note that I didn't drag them into my goals; I created goals that pushed me to spend intentional, quality time with them). In the end I had the three categories: Family & Social, Business & Personal Development, and Fitness & Adventure.

The categories showed me if I had weighted my challenge too heavily in one area over another, but that by itself wasn't enough.

That's because some goals are simply more significant than others. Taking my daughter on a special weekend getaway isn't the same as going to the movies. There is a difference in time, financial, and emotional impact. (This is where my inner-nerd and consulting experience kicks in to develop weighting formulas in Excel. You don't have to do that; just make sure it's generally in balance.)

As you categorize the goals, some may merge into one and others may split between categories. This is normal and is part of the process. You may kill some (move them to a holding area vs. deleting them because they may come back or spawn better ideas). Continue to review them until you narrow the list down to the number you decided to do in your challenge.

Wordsmithing Your Goals

It's important that your goals are written properly. If they are vague, their meaning may shift in the time between when you start and when you finish. This is *your* challenge and how rigid or flexible you make it is up to you. And while flexibility is important to me (see the next section), so is integrity. This isn't the same as your work integrity; this is the integrity of the challenge for yourself. High standards will result in a more meaningful journey and ultimately a more meaningful experience when you cross the finish line.

If you do create a goal with wiggle room, do it on purpose. I had running a 5K on my list, but was ~~bullied~~ encouraged by Jody and Steve Berkey to add in a half marathon. I really didn't know if I was up to 13.1 miles, based on the time required to train, the impact on my body, or my own commitment to seeing it through.

I didn't want to add anything to the list just for the sake of adding it or knowing I would fail before I started (if I even bothered to start it). So my goal was "*Attempt* a Half Marathon" instead of "*Complete* a Half Marathon." I knew that an honest attempt was within my control. So I trained for thirteen weeks and started the half marathon. By giving it an honest bit of effort, I had accomplished the goal, and finishing the race was a wonderful bonus!

Grading Your Goals

Many people follow the SMART or SMARTER mnemonic[3] for assessing the quality of a goal. You can use those systems or anything else you like. For me the key things are:

Specificity – Are you clear about what the goal is and when it can be considered accomplished (measured as complete, deadline-driven, etc.)? Would another person see it the same as you do? Don't leave room for confusion.

Personal Ownership – This may be the most important aspect, if I had to pick just one. You aren't doing this challenge because someone else is forcing you. It doesn't work that way. You are doing this because you want to. That's why defining your motivation in Step One is so important. You will push harder if you own your goals.

---

[3] http://en.wikipedia.org/wiki/SMART_criteria

Realistic But Ambitious – You need to push yourself to accomplish real goals with real results. Success or failure is ultimately less important than the growth you gain through the process. But if your goals are simply impossible, it will be too easy to quit when it gets hard because good enough doesn't exist. Aim high, but make sure the laws of time and space still apply.

Wild Cards

I am a firm believer in flexibility and built it into my challenge. A year is a long time and things change. While I knew I was going to have a total of forty goals on my list, I decided to leave five of them blank at the start. This left room for new opportunities to show up on my radar, and some did.

Consider leaving a few open slots on your list, depending on your timeline and need for creative flexibility. Just be careful: if you have more than a few wild cards, you risk missing out on the intentionality of the challenge.

The Rules of the Challenge

It's important to establish some basic rules for your challenge. Without rules, you risk your level of personal commitment. You are the master of the challenge, but you need something to stick to or you'll change it to fit your situation instead of pushing yourself to change.

In 40 Before 40, I had some simple ground rules that gave me flexibility. The wild-card goals allowed me to add new and interesting opportunities as they presented themselves. I also allowed for substitutions. I had some goals that were tied to specific dates or locations. If the opportunity closed for a legitimate reason, I didn't want to have to call it a failure.

You can address this to a degree in how you write your goals, but I wanted to have that ability without feeling like I was cheating, so I set it as a rule from the beginning. It also kept some fun in the mix, because I didn't want it to feel like forced labor.

Ultimately, you're in charge of your challenge and you can do whatever you want. But some basic ground rules at the beginning will help keep you on track.

Assess the Types

As I worked though my challenge, I realized that my goals could be one of three types:

One-Time – These goals are driven by an event and are all-or-nothing goals. The event happens and the goal is either completed or not completed. This sounds simple, and some of these types of goals are simple to complete, but some require a lot of preparation and work in order to get to the event.

An example would be completing a marathon. The event is when you cross the finish line. But if you don't prepare, it probably won't happen. You could even train for months and start the race, but fail to finish and therefore fail to complete the goal.

Incremental – These goals require regular action over a protracted period of time, perhaps even daily effort. You'll definitely want to record your progress along the way, both as an encouragement and because you may not be able to see the finish line any other way. These are the kind of goals that can be measured in percent complete.

An example would be reading the Bible over the course of a year. At 1,200 pages, you would be able to plot a graph showing progress at 100 pages per month. By tracking how far along you are at any moment, you can see if you are ahead of or behind schedule.

Incremental goals are good for establishing new habits, but they can bite you if you don't stay on top of them. In addition to cramming half your reading into the last week of the year to meet your goal (if you even do), you'll miss out on the point of reading in the first place. Aim to stay ahead of the curve and build a little cushion while meeting the intent of the goal.

Collection – These goals are made up of a subset of smaller goals. Progress on these goals may be irregular, but they too can stack up to the point that they become impossible or meaningless.

An example would be a goal to have twelve dates with your spouse over the course of a year, or to create ten products. You may have some months with two or three, and other months with none. Consistency is great but not always possible with these goals, so stay on top of them or the deadline will sneak up on you.

Count the Cost: Budget and Time

As you look over your list of goals, you may want to factor in the impact of time and money. Ask yourself how much it will cost to accomplish each goal and if it's possible and/or worth the effort.

A collection of worthy individual goals can easily create chaos when taken as a whole. This can happen when your business goals take time away from your family or prevent your family goals from being achieved. Use a balanced approach.

The same thing happens with your finances. When I totaled up what it would take to accomplish my 40 Before 40 Challenge, the result was around ten thousand dollars. Some of those costs had been planned, but some had not. I had to make adjustments and find creative ways to meet the intent of a goal, even if the goal itself had to shift.

In the end, it was worth the effort and I found a way to make things work. But if your goals include expensive trips all over the world, you better know how to pay for it, or the goals are unrealistic.

Step Four: Track Your Time and Tasks

You Need a Calendar

You probably already have a calendar. Maybe it's the one hanging on the wall in your office or kitchen, or maybe it's on your phone or computer. You'll need to pull it out because time is a significant factor when you're doing a challenge like this.

You'll need to review key dates. There may already be activities on your calendar that are a part of your challenge, conflict with your challenge, or even spark ideas for your challenge. Whatever the length of your challenge, having an up-to-date calendar is absolutely required. The format and type of calendar is up to you.

Using Your Calendar

There is a critical feature built into all calendars and it's called The Future! All calendars can see into the future and while there are no absolute guarantees that what you place on a future date will happen, your odds go up significantly when those forecasted events are documented.

So if one of your goals is a date night with your spouse planned for April 13th, put it on your calendar. This kind of planning is crucial to being intentional with your time during your challenge. It makes it hard to forget (if you review your calendar!) and it builds anticipation (both the exciting kind for things you're looking forward to, and the nervous kind for things you have to prepare for).

Another way to use the calendar to your advantage is to include the time you need to work on your challenge goals as a part of your regular schedule. Make these appointments with yourself and don't break them any more easily than you would an appointment with another person.

If you have a running goal, schedule your training runs. If you have a reading goal, schedule your reading times. If you have it on your schedule, it greatly increases your odds of success.

The Tangible Calendar

I love my electronic devices. With one click, I can add an appointment to my Google calendar and have it instantly appear on my iPhone, iPad, laptops, desktops, and anything else with access to the Internet.

But sometimes I need something tangible. I want a physical calendar hanging on my wall that I can look at and write on with a pen or pencil (or a Sharpie!). And until I can afford a touchscreen that turns on when I gaze upon it, I'm going old school!

The concept for a Tangible Calendar comes from my friend, Jonathan Pool. I was visiting his home in Michigan, going through an intensive two-day LifePlan (I highly recommend doing a LifePlan and Jonathan is a great facilitator/coach!). He had a full-year calendar printed out and hung on a makeshift room divider. Anyone can do that—the magic was his planning system.

If he had a goal of conducting 10 LifePlans that year, he would have 10 sticky notes on the side of the calendar. When one was scheduled, he would move it onto the calendar. He also did this for family events and personal goals.

With one glance at his calendar, Jonathan had an instant and tangible reminder of his goals and the progress he was making on his goals. I took a picture of his setup to inspire a version of my own.[4]

Today in my office I have two magnetic whiteboards hanging on the wall. Each holds six months of a printed calendar. I use tiny magnets instead of sticky notes. All of my calendar-based goals are printed, cut into day-sized rectangles, and attached to the whiteboard below the calendar pages. When a goal is scheduled or accomplished, it goes on the calendar for that day. I can touch it. I can see it. And that makes all my goals a bit more real than when they are just bouncing around in my head.

You Need a Tracker

Remember when you were creating your list in Step Two? You had to pick some kind of tool to document your list of goals. I recommend a good spreadsheet, but paper, whiteboards, and other tools also work well.

At this point you've refined your list. You have a number of goals and they are categorized. You are serious about your challenge and you are ready to begin. However, if you fail to track your goals along

---

[4] See pictures of my tangible calendar at
http://conqueryourkryptonite.com/tangible-calendar/

the way, you risk getting to the end of your challenge and wondering what happened.

Measurement of your progress is another critical factor in success. There is something encouraging about checking off a goal and knowing that you accomplished something that you set out to do.

If all of your goals are one-time, all-or-nothing goals, then it's simple. You check them off when you do them and leave them unchecked until you do.

But it's likely you'll have some incremental and collection goals as well (and some of those one-time goals take a lot of effort to achieve). Tracking your progress on these kinds of goals serves two purposes.

First, you stay on top of your progress. You won't have to keep the data in your head and wonder if you've read ten books or twelve books toward your goal of reading fifty-two books in a year.

Second, you'll get a reminder each and every time you make an update or review your progress. It's hard to read forty books in the last month of your challenge. Failing to track your goals increases the odds of failure.

What Should You Track

Everyone's challenge will be different, but here's how I would recommend setting up a basic spreadsheet:

Column A – ID Number

Column B – Goal Name or Title

Column C – Category

Column D – Type (One-Time, Incremental, Collection)

Column E – Estimated Budget or Cost

Column F – Estimated Completion Date

Column G – Actual Completion Date

Column H – Status

Column I – Notes/Updates

ID	Goal	Category	Type	Budget	End Date	Actual Date	Status	Notes/Updates
1	12 Date Nights	Family and Social	Collection	$ 300	12/31		In Process	2 complete
2	Family Service Project	Family and Social	One-Time	$ -	3/10		Scheduled	Litter pickup on 3/10
3	Read 20 Books	Family and Social	Collection	$ 200	12/31		In Process	4 complete
4	Teach FPU Class	Biz/Personal Dev	One-Time	$ -	6/14		Scheduled	Scheduled for 6/14 start date
5	Start a podcast	Biz/Personal Dev	One-Time	$ 300	12/31	3/1	Completed	Launched 3/1
6	Join Mastermind Group	Biz/Personal Dev	One-Time	$ -	12/31		Not Started	Searching
7	Walk Two Million Steps	Fitness/Adventure	Incremental	$ -	12/31		In Process	200K as of 2/28
8	Finish Spartan Race	Fitness/Adventure	One-Time	$ 100	7/1		Scheduled	Entry fee paid
9	Attend NASCAR Race	Fitness/Adventure	One-Time	$ 250	9/6		Scheduled	Planning trip for Labor Day
10	TBD	Wildcard			12/31		Not Started	

Example spreadsheet

Visit ChallengeAccepted.info for additional resources and templates.

This kind of setup is ideal for one-time goals. It's as easy as entering a completion date when it's done.

For the simple incremental or collection goals, you can make notes to document your progress and update the status accordingly, but not call it complete until it's finished. More complex goals may need their own tracking sheet to document detailed progress along the way.

A simple goal might be reading 12 books in one year. You can put the title of each book in the notes field as you complete them.

A more complex goal might be walking 10,000 steps a day for 75% of the days in your challenge. If you use a Fitbit or some other kind of pedometer, the data may be stored online, but you'll still need to review your progress on a regular basis and keep track of the days when you met the goal and the days you didn't. This is where I would simply add another tab on my spreadsheet, create a column for dates and another for steps, then record my daily totals on that tab.

I actually did this for my "two million steps in 2013" goal. My spreadsheet had a dedicated tab with every day of the year on it and my steps for each day were entered there. It calculated my progress, showed a line graph comparing actual to plan, color-coded days as good or bad, and even calculated the number of steps per day I still needed to hit in order to reach my goal by the end of the year. Again, I'm a nerd! Don't do this unless you are as well.

Think forward a bit while setting up your tracker so that you're capturing the needed data from the beginning. But don't over-complicate this like I tend to do (see above, I'm crazy). You can do this in a simple 99-cent notebook or three-ring binder dedicated to your challenge, using the front pages as the overall checklist, and a few pages as needed for detailed tracking. Tracking is important, but not more important than your goals, so do what works for you and supports you as you do the work.

Make it Visible

Even if you use a spreadsheet, you need to have a printed version of your goals posted somewhere you can see it. Make it look nice. Be creative and artistic if that's a talent of yours.

Post it on the bathroom mirror or your refrigerator door. You'll want to see the reminder often (daily). The idea is that seeing boxes checked off—and knowing the stories behind them—will encourage you to keep going.

Step Five: Add Accountability

Find a Partner

Nothing will sink your challenge faster than trying to do it alone and/or in secret. You need someone who believes in what you're doing to cheer you on and even get disappointed if you fail or give up (failing is almost always okay; giving up rarely is).

By inviting another person into your journey, you are honoring them. You are giving them permission to bust your butt, and that means you trust and respect them.

Choose wisely. If the person is a pushover, they may not hold you accountable properly. If they are a bully, they will simply beat you up. Find someone who has a vested interest in your success (they love you, care about you, respect you) and will be honest with you even if the truth hurts. They need to be part cheerleader and part coach.

Sometimes your spouse can be an accountability partner. It depends on you and your spouse. It could also be a friend or family member, or even another person who is doing the challenge with you. If you need more than one accountability partner, that's fine.

Sharing Your Journey

Having an accountability partner is one way to share the incredible journey you're about to begin. Another way is to share it with a larger group of friends or even the entire world!

You can create a blog, or post on your existing blog. You can make a commitment to post weekly updates on Facebook. Get creative and see if you can find the accountability you need with some extra encouragement by going public. You might even inspire some others to join you, making you a leader, a trendsetter, and an all-around better person!

One word of caution about this: depending on the goal and your personality, sharing with too large an audience may lower your odds of success. The reason is that when you put a big goal out there, people can be impressed and you get praise and pats on the back before ever really doing anything. Some goals may be better off shared with a smaller, encouraging audience or partner who will feed the process instead of your ego.

I learned about this danger zone from Michael Hyatt[5] after I'd fallen into the trap with my first book. I promised it would be done in six months, and that turned into three years! There were other factors involved, but this contributed to my lack of intense production.

Do It Together

Another powerful way to enter into a challenge and complete it is to do it with other people. You don't have to have the same goals, but a similar timeline would help.

Organize a group of friends or co-workers. Do it as a part of your Sunday school class or social club. Or invite a group of online strangers to join you, and make new friends. All you have to do is create the opportunity and share it. Create a theme or a shared purpose and then be the leader. Make being a group

---

[5] I don't remember exactly when I heard Michael Hyatt mention this concept about goals, but he did write about it in a blog post (http://michaelhyatt.com/should-you-keep-your-goals-to-yourself.html), where he referenced a 2010 Derek Sivers TED Talk that referenced several research studies.

leader one of your goals if that's what it takes. And if you want everyone who joins your group to buy this book, I won't argue with you (you're the group leader!).

**Visit ChallengeAccepted.info for
free group leadership guides and tools
to help organize a *Challenge Accepted!* experience.**

Another place this can work is at home. I can easily see families sitting down and working on a list of individual and group goals. Kids of all ages can participate, though younger ones may need more help to know what's realistic, and older ones may need more guidance regarding what's appropriate. This would be an incredible summer activity to keep them learning and doing something productive instead of sleeping late or watching television and playing video games all day.

If setting up a group is not an option, then look for opportunities to link individual goals with groups of people. There is no way I would have completed a half marathon in 2013 if it weren't for Steve and Jody Berkey's 13-in-13 Half Marathon

Challenge. They linked together wannabe runners from all over the world in a Facebook group. The encouragement, education, and accountability were exactly what I needed to be successful with one of my most difficult goals.

CHAPTER THREE:
It's Time to Get Serious

◆

*It is not the critic who counts; not the man who points out how the strong man stumbles, or where the doer of deeds could have done them better. The credit belongs to the man who is actually **in the arena**, whose face is marred by dust and sweat and blood; who strives valiantly; who errs, who comes short again and again, because there is no effort without error and shortcoming; but who does actually strive to do the deeds; who knows great enthusiasms, the great devotions; who spends himself in a worthy cause; who at the best knows in the end the triumph of high achievement, and who at the worst, if he fails, at least fails while daring greatly, so that his place shall never be with those cold and timid souls who neither know victory nor defeat.*

— Theodore Roosevelt

New Year's Resolutions Don't Work

It's not really a surprise that New Year's resolutions don't work, is it? The idea is fairly ridiculous to begin with.

Pick some goal that you've ignored the last eleven months. Start on January 1st and see how far you get into the New Year. When you fail after a few days or weeks, give up and wait until next year to try again.

It's not just ridiculous—it's insane! If the goal is important to you, why would you wait another ten or eleven months to start again? Because it's hard?

I get that a new year is bright and shiny and full of potential. I get that it can inspire you to try new things and I'm all for that. However, you can do that on May 26th or July 11th just as easily.

It's more about your mindset than the calendar. I don't care when you pick up and read this book. I hope sales in December and January are great. But whenever you're reading this, decide to begin documenting your challenge today and start doing it within a week or so, not months from now.

Enter the Arena

If you don't enter the arena and participate in life, you cannot win. It's as simple as that. You have to risk getting bloody, getting hurt, failing in some capacity—or victory cannot be called victory.

The arena is the only place where victory exists. You can dream and plan all you want. But if you don't enter the field of battle, you are just an observer of life and subject to whatever spoils accidentally land on your plate.

However, if you become a participant, you have a chance at success. You have to have a plan and you have to train, but would you rather exist fully-alive on the arena floor or sitting on the couch watching other people live real lives?

Sadly, that's a lot of our existence these days. TV, especially "reality" television, allows us to partake in virtual experiences. We can live vicariously through other people. That has its place as a temporary escape or respite from battle, but I want the scars and the stories that come from real life and real adventure. You can't get those watching television.

The Floor of the Arena

The arena is a metaphor for real life, and in reality, it is as much a playground as it is a battleground. It's where you struggle to achieve something that you desire or something you simply must bring into existence.

It can be an office cubicle, or a racetrack, or a stage. It can be a computer screen, or a canvas, or a kitchen. Maybe it's even a living room (as long as the TV isn't on all the time!).

In the context of *Challenge Accepted!*, it's where you put in the effort to achieve your goals.

Running a half marathon? The arena is your mindset, your training, and eventually the city streets where you run the race.

Writing a book? The arena is your screen or typewriter, your office or coffeehouse, and it's even your alarm clock telling you when to start and stop.

Growing a business? The arena is your community, and hopefully it's a happy hunting ground where you can bring back more than a day's meal before the sun goes down.

The Professional vs. The Amateur

This new mindset is what separates the couch potatoes from the warriors. Amateurs are welcome to apply, but they better turn pro fast.

You have to be a professional, even if your pursuit is outside the realm of business. Take the arena and your efforts seriously. A professional mindset is critical to your ultimate success or failure.

This is why it's so important for the goals of your challenge to be *your* goals and not someone else's goals for you. Personal ownership is one of the hallmarks of a professional.

But this doesn't mean you can't have fun. Hard work is fun when you're working toward something you care about. So have fun. Have lots of fun. Just make sure you're doing the right things with the right attitude and you will.

Your Manifesto

What Exactly is a Manifesto?

According to Merriam-Webster online, a manifesto is "a written statement declaring publicly the intentions, motives, or views of its issuer."[6]

I like this definition because it addresses three key components of the *Challenge Accepted!* concept:

Written Statement – When you write something down, you take it from a thought or idea in your head and make it tangible and shareable. It can stare back at you and it can shout to others. A brain surgeon can't pull it out of your head via surgery. You have to write it down!

Declaring Publicly – This part of the definition reiterates the concept of sharing your ideas, and, to a degree, the accountability aspect of your challenge. At the very least, by making your challenge public, you are taking ownership of and responsibility for it. That takes guts and it takes purposeful thought.

---

[6] "Manifesto." *Merriam-Webster.com*. Merriam-Webster, n.d. Web. 20 Jan. 2015. <http://www.merriam-webster.com/dictionary/manifesto>.

Intentions...of Its Issuer – Again, this section is all about personal ownership and responsibility. The challenge is *your* challenge and the motives are *yours*. Others may not agree with you or support you, but that's okay. You're not doing it because they want you to do it. You're doing it for yourself.

Writing Your Manifesto

Your manifesto doesn't have to be long, and it certainly doesn't have to be signed in blood.

In its simplest form, your manifesto is a restatement of the reason you are doing the challenge. What is your purpose? What is your mission?

Write it down, post it where you'll see it every day, and own it.

Use a sticky note or a scrap of paper. Tape it to the bathroom mirror or refrigerator door along with your list of goals. Be creative and make it pretty, or make it ugly so it stares back at you, daring you to take it seriously.

Put it on your computer monitor or make a custom desktop background. Don't hide it from your co-workers or family. Make it so that when they notice it (and they should), they ask what it is and you can invite them into the cult (just kidding about that last part, but do encourage them to start their own challenge and buy the book!).

CHAPTER FOUR:
Enjoy Your Journey

◆

It is good to have an end to journey toward, but it is the journey that matters in the end.

— **Ursula K. Le Guin**

The Journey Matters

All great stories involve a journey of some kind, and the best parts of the story happen on the journey. That's because simply going from Point A to Point B is boring!

The journey is where the action takes place. It's where you struggle and fight, where conflicts emerge, and where everything that really matters happens.

Let's explore a few famous stories and boil them down to Point A and Point B (spoiler warning):

Star Wars – An orphan named Luke who lives on a desert planet ends up getting a medal with some new friends.

The Hobbit – A short guy named Bilbo leaves his home and comes back with a ring.

Lord of the Rings – Another short guy, this one named Frodo, leaves his home with a ring and comes back without it.

National Lampoon's Vacation – A man takes his family on vacation from Chicago to California and comes home.

Rocky – A boxer gets in a prizefight and loses.

Rocky II – A boxer gets in a prizefight and wins.

This is fun! I could do it all day, and I bet you could, too. Boil any great story down to A and B and you'll have a movie that's not worth watching or a book that's not worth reading. If it were a life, it might not be worth living.

The great news is that life *is* worth living because we live it in the middle of A and B, where all of the interesting stuff takes place. Some of it sucks, and some of it is great, and along the way we end up with some amazing stories to tell.

Life is made up of journeys, not just destinations. We boil it down to the destinations in history books and obituaries, but real stories from real people are all about the journey.

Challenge Accepted! is, in part, about helping you tell some great stories—and not a recap of a story you saw or read, but one you lived to the fullest!

Don't Just Check the Boxes

Caught Up in the Journey

The journey can be long and hard and still be ignored. When I'm driving seven hundred miles from Alabama to Missouri to visit my parents, I'm not that concerned with the interesting things I see along the way. I just want to get there as quickly as possible (without getting a ticket).

Yet every time I make the drive, I pass Exit 5 in Memphis. It's hard to miss because of all the signs directing you to visit Graceland, the legendary home of Elvis Presley. I've always wanted to go, but I've never taken that exit. The journey is so long I just want it to be over.

But as I sit here writing, I feel the tinge of regret that comes from missing out on an adventure. I'm going to have to find a way to visit Graceland soon.

Waking Up on the Journey

Not all of my trips to and from my parents' home are so mundane. I've learned to enjoy the sites along the way (like the giant raven statue in Ravenden, Arkansas), and I have fun crunching trip numbers like estimating time-to-arrival or maximizing miles per gallon.

A few years ago my wife couldn't make the trip, so I loaded the kids in the car and away we went. I love my kids and I try to be Super Dad, but I was pretty much dreading twelve hours in the car. Not all journeys are fun!

Yet I remember we had a great time. Their behavior was above average, and a bit past Memphis I decided to change our plan on the fly. We had left early in the morning and were making good time. Though it would add a few hours to our trip, getting out of the car for a little while would be refreshing.

I took a detour from our well-known path and headed to Batesville, Arkansas. Batesville is the home of one of my heroes, NASCAR driver Mark Martin. He has a museum at his car dealership and it was fascinating. It had cars, trophies, uniforms— everything from his amazing career in racing. (Oh, and I had promised the kids ice cream if they were up for adding a few hours to our trip.)

It was an intentional deviation from a very routine family road trip for the Woosley's. We saw an opportunity and we took it. Now we have a collection of happy memories, some fun family photos, and a few souvenirs from the gift shop.

Sometimes you have to wake up in the middle of a journey. Far too often we're on automatic pilot, especially if we're traveling roads we've traveled before. Do something different and break out of the routine.

You'll need to do the same thing on the journey to work your challenge. Otherwise you risk getting so caught up in checking off goals that you miss the point of the whole thing.

Remember your motivation. Remember your purpose. Remember your manifesto.

What Happens on the Journey

Like Going to Grandma's House

It's pretty unlikely that your journey will be a straight, flat trip from A to B. It'll have twists and turns, and you may just have to go over the river and through the woods to get to where you want to go!

It's okay to have expectations; just don't make them all good or all bad.

Easy Sailing and Coasting

For all the talk of angst and conflict and the messy middle, there will be times when the journey is easy. All you have to do is show up and things get done both efficiently and effectively. Everything you touch turns to gold and you're the life of the party. Enjoy it when it happens, but don't expect it to last long.

Those are the rare days, and you should be thankful that they are rare because those aren't the days when great stories are made. If they aren't rare, you're probably not trying hard enough. You can only coast when you're going downhill.

Conflicts, Setbacks, and Overwhelm

Now we're getting into some real adventure! This is

where the hard work takes place, and any goal worth doing will require some hard work.

Some days you will feel like you're going backward and failing. Some days you *will be* failing! But that's okay and you have to learn to be okay with failing on the way to a worthy goal. If the destination has significance and you've turned pro, you can get up the next day and keep going.

Resolving, Advancing, and Overcoming

Now we get to the really exciting and rewarding part of the journey. The conflict you faced has been resolved and you're advancing faster than ever before. You've overcome the obstacles and challenges that slowed you down, and the finish line is just around the corner.

When I ran my first (and so far only) half marathon in 2013, it was the Marine Corps Historic Half in Fredericksburg, Virginia. The first ten miles were pretty flat, and then I came to the two-mile vertical segment called Hospital Hill. It's probably only a speed bump when you're driving, but it kicked my butt. Eventually it leveled out and I could see the finish line. It's hard to describe what the last 100 yards felt like. And the victory was sweeter because of that hill.

See how the difficulty and the challenge created a better story?

The elements of the journey—not the destination—are what give a story its heartbeat. Without the tension of a challenge, your story will have no flavor.

Being Present

Wake Up

It's easy to go through life and miss the important moments. In retrospect, what we thought was important at the beginning changes because of what we learned on the journey.

Parents look back on their lives and realize they missed the kids' growing up because they were busy at work.

Students hate school until they graduate and realize it was a special time of learning and friendship that will probably never happen again.

We all look back and have regrets. We regret saying "no" when we should have said "yes," or saying "yes" when we should have said "no." There are mistakes and failures we wish we could take back and do over. But we can't stay in the past.

We also can't live only in the future or we'll miss out on what's happening right now, which will then become our past when we get to the future and have even more regret!

Time-Orientation

Without getting too philosophical or scientific, our lives have three relationships with time: the past, the present, and the future.

While we acknowledge all three, I believe we all have a tendency to focus on one of them more than the others.

Some people are living in the past. Their present is focused on things that have happened already. It may be good things or bad things, but they cannot overcome the past in the present. It sticks with them and controls them.

We all have a past and we should be thankful for it. What happened in our past shapes us and teaches us. But we have to apply the lessons of the past in the present. You can choose to let a negative past experience help you overcome, or let it chain you down.

Others have a future orientation, always looking forward and anticipating something that does not yet exist. They can be optimistic or pessimistic about the future. Either way, it affects their present.

I tend to be an optimistic futurist. I see the future as something bright and shiny and full of infinite possibility. The problem is that my mind can spend so much time in the future (or trying to create it) that I fail to notice and enjoy the present.

Even at this very moment, I'm writing these words and my mind is thinking about finishing the book, designing the cover, inviting people to purchase and read it, getting it printed, hoping Oprah notices and shares with her fans, making the best-seller lists, and going on an international book-signing tour.

See, optimistic AND futuristic!

I have to wake up and realize that I'm dreaming. Some of that will happen and it'll be great. Some won't and that'll be okay. But right now—in this moment—I have to focus on this sentence and these words and these letters. I have to focus so that my message is clear, and I have to realize that I'm doing something I love to do. I have to be awake in the present. I love writing and I love being a writer. There should be a huge smile on my face right now (except I'm still thinking about Oprah).

Find a Trigger

It is hard for people to live in the present. Some do it better than others, but we all have a past and a future. The past is stable and sticky; the future is new and shiny. If you have any worries about your challenge, this should be your chief concern: that you get so focused on checking off boxes that you forget to enjoy the ride. There is fun to be had in the process and along the journey.

Find a way to bring yourself into the present. This is especially important at the beginning of your challenge and as you approach the work of each item on your list. Say a prayer. Create a mantra. Commit to reminding others of the moment and invite them to remind you. Now is now and will never be again. Enjoy now.

One of the ways I was able to help ground myself in the moment was to keep a journal. All of the data tracking helped a bit, but could easily become a chore that reinforced box checking. But the journal forced me to slow down and capture the story of each of the challenges on my list. Doing so helped me notice more in the moment and enjoy the act of *doing* as much as the act of *accomplishing*. There's a difference and it's important. Being aware will also help you document the story better in your journal, and you'll end up with a self-feeding, positive cycle for journaling and living in the moment.

Document the Journey

When it comes to documenting your challenge, you are limited only by the bounds of your imagination and budget.

Journal – Go out and purchase a $10 basic journal at the bookstore or a $100 handcrafted, leather-bound journal from a specialty shop. As long as you are willing to write in it and capture the stories from your journey (both good and bad), you'll be able to relive and share your adventure for decades.

Blog – Whether it's a public blog or a private document on your computer, blogging is just as good as a hand-written journal when it comes to capturing your stories. I tend to write more while typing, so this fits me better. The added benefit over a journal is that it's much easier to share, and can even be formatted and printed into a book.

Pictures – Not every goal in your challenge will have a visual element. Yet pictures are awesome for those that can be captured, and they can easily be incorporated into a journal or blog. Get creative and have fun. With today's cellphone cameras, you have no excuse for missing out on great photos along the way.

Remember that the purpose of documenting the journey is to capture your stories and emotions, and, ultimately, to help you be present along the way.

Visit ChallengeAccepted.info for information about sharing your *Challenge Accepted!* experience. Submit your blogs or photos and join the movement.

Remember to Celebrate!

I don't care how small, how simple, or how easy some of your goals are; they all deserve an appropriate celebration when they are accomplished.

But they don't all deserve a full-blown party. After all, I said "appropriate."

So give yourself a high-five. Enjoy a small reward. Breathe in your victory and smile for a moment of triumph.

If the goal was really big, or you've completed the journey and arrived at your destination, throw a party. Have a parade in your honor (even if it's only through the living room or the neighbor's front yard).

The point is to celebrate. You set out to do something and you did it. You followed through and probably changed your life (and others') in some way.

And if there were some failures along the way, if the list is incomplete and the deadline has come and gone, celebrate anyway.

That's right: celebrate anyway!

The failures are lessons learned. They are attempts at something new that didn't work out, or attempts you didn't take that stare back at you, forcing regret to bubble up from your heart—and you'll learn something from that as well.

Remember, it's about the journey. Most of our goals won't be a matter of life or death. They're about living life. If you've done that, then celebrate!

Visit ChallengeAccepted.info for free resources, templates, and group leadership guides to help you take on your challenge and lead others into theirs.

EPILOGUE

At the beginning of the book, I mentioned my father's Air Force retirement ceremony. I was a 19-year-old college freshman and he was a 39-year-old Chief Master Sergeant. I was proud of him and his service. So I wrote him this poem called "Standing Down" and read it at the ceremony:

Many have stood where you stand today.
Standing with Distinction, Honor, & Pride.

Your battles were fought and your battles were won.
They were won with Distinction, Honor, & Pride.

Now the future seems so uncertain, and the man that stood up for what was right, must part with the vehicle that has carried him here.
It was fueled with Distinction, Honor, & Pride.

Today the man must begin again.
His uncertainty is unfounded, because again, he will succeed.

He will succeed with Distinction, Honor, & Pride.

Reading this poem twenty-two years later stirs up a lot of emotion and memories. He is still my hero and had the greatest influence on my life.

"Standing down" is a term used when someone steps away from a leadership position or a state of alertness.

My father was taking off his uniform and leaving the profession of military service, to which he had dedicated more than half of his life. But he wasn't going to sit in a rocking chair at thirty-nine. He wasn't going to stop being my father. He was standing down one thing to stand up another.

That is what I want you to do.

Stand down from the accidental life. Stop going through the motions and take control of the things you've left on autopilot.

Stand up and be alert to the world around you. There are people depending on you. They need your wisdom and your brilliance, your smile and your art.

Step into the journey of living an intentional life by taking on a challenge. Whether you succeed or fail doesn't matter as much as the change it will cause inside of you. I firmly believe it will make you a better person.

Two Voices

I imagine there are two voices in your head at this moment. The first is negative or neutral. It says, "You can't do this" or "Why bother?"

It tells you that your dreams or goals are improbable, if not impossible. It tries to diminish your spark of excitement by saying this is for other people, not you.

"While the book is good and the concept is interesting, it's something you can't do right now, but maybe later (if ever)."

"Wait until you're forty, then do it," or "You already turned forty, so you missed your chance. Sorry."

The second voice might be muffled under the droning on of the first voice. You may struggle to hear it if the first voice is strong.

It's saying, "Please."

It's saying, "Yes."

It's saying, "I want to do this. I need to do this."

If you feed the second voice just for a moment, it will get louder. Then you'll hear it rise above the first voice like a thunderbird.

"I will do this!"

"Tell me it can't be done!"

"Dare me to do it!"

"I will prove you wrong!"

The challenge is yours to craft and to tame. Your journey is about to begin.

Accept the challenge and make it legendary.

Visit ChallengeAccepted.info for free resources, templates, and group leadership guides to help you take on your challenge and lead others into theirs.

APPENDIX

My 40 Before 40 List

Below is a simple listing of the categories and goals I set for my 40 Before 40 Challenge. It may serve as a bit of inspiration for your goals, but don't copy it or let it do all the work. Make your challenge your own!

Family and Social
1) Daddy/Daughter Getaway
2) Father/Son Event
3) Teach Ian to ride a bike
4) Get gloves and play catch with Anna and Ian
5) Host a party
6) Have a getaway weekend with Heather
7) Start recycling
8) Have a family service project
9) Visit a museum or attend a symphony/play/opera
10) Family Vacation
11) Read the entire Bible
12) Twelve Dates with My Wife
13) Visit Congress or AL Legislature

Business and Personal Development
14) Publish my first book
15) Produce ten products (e-books, audio programs, etc.)
16) Conduct group coaching course
17) Conduct first STRATOP
18) Finish my office
19) Establish LLC
20) Start a podcast
21) Consistently wake up between 5 and 6 am

22) Teach a community class (other than FPU)
23) Join/Start Local Mastermind/Networking Group
24) Make 100 blog posts

Fitness and Adventure

25) Ride a Century (100-mile single bike event)
26) Complete first 5K race
27) Drive a race car
28) Complete second Spartan race
29) Attend a NASCAR event
30) Take a firearms safety class
31) BMI 25 or less
32) Complete a fast
33) Record two million steps in 2013
34) Complete the Manitou Springs Incline
35) Ride over 1200 miles

Wildcards

36) Wildcard #1
37) Wildcard #2
38) Wildcard #3
39) Wildcard #4
40) Wildcard #5

My 40 Before 40 Results

As I worked through my challenge in 2013, I posted updates on the 8th of each month. Below is a summary of the final results from January 8th, 2014. Some basic editing has been done and some additional context has been added since the original post (including some updates on what happened in the following year).

Key: ☑ Win | ☒ Loss | ☐ Draw

◆

Family and Social

☑ **1) Daddy/Daughter Getaway**

Plan: My daughter Anna and I started taking an annual weekend trip a few summers ago. I really look forward to these trips and I know she does, too! This year we may end up surfing in Cocoa Beach if she gets her wish.

Actual: Plans for Cocoa Beach and Atlanta didn't work out, but we had a fantastic Daddy-Daughter date night on November 15th. I'm hopeful we can make a big weekend trip for 2014, along with many date nights!

Note: In July of 2014, we ended up spending a weekend in Tampa, visiting my brother and going to a Paramore/Fall Out Boy concert. We had a lot of date nights as well.

☑ 2) Father/Son Event

Plan: I want to start a similar tradition with my son, Ian. Going to a monster truck rally may suffice. Boys are easier in that regard!

Actual: On July 5th, Ian and I took in the new *Man of Steel* movie, followed by sushi with Pop Rocks (surprisingly good!). A few weeks later we also made a guys-only trip from Alabama to Missouri for my grandfather's 80th birthday. Good times!

☑ 3) Teach Ian to ride a bike

Plan: The biking bug bit me hard last year and I have some big events planned for 2013 (see below). But one of the biggies is getting my son on his bike. He's frozen with fear, but I know he'll love it once he figures it out.

Actual: I honestly don't know how it happened considering the numerous attempts and meltdowns through the years. But on September 8th, 2013, Ian finally did it! Once. Just that once. And then, to my surprise, and with one little push, in December he did it again. He stopped, restarted himself, and now he can truly ride his bike!

☑ 4) Get gloves and play catch with Anna and Ian

Plan: I grew up playing baseball and loved playing catch with my brother and sister, neighborhood kids, my father, and even my mom! This will get us outside, active, and together.

Actual: We went to the sports supply store one day and got gloves and tennis balls. We played a little catch at the park, and that was about it. But later we did use the balls for a few rounds of driveway tennis. It's a start and I'll call it a win.

☒ 5) Host a party

Plan: I'm a bit of an introvert so I have no idea how this will manifest itself, but I'm up to the challenge.

Actual: Well, it didn't manifest. I was hoping to have a big birthday blowout, but birthdays on Wednesdays just after the holidays aren't easy to pull off. It's my fault for not being more proactive. I definitely want to host some smaller dinner parties soon. Who wants to come over?

☐ 6) Have a getaway weekend with Heather

Plan: Heather is my wife. She is an amazing mother, and probably 10 times better than I at parenting. But she deserves a break and we need to have an escape together. It'll be good for our marriage, which is good for the kids (even if they don't want us to go!).

Actual: We celebrated our 17th anniversary in September 2013, but the schedule just didn't allow for a getaway then. Before we knew it, the year was over. However, we are going away very, very soon. We just didn't meet the birthday deadline. I'll call it a draw!

Note: We had a great getaway two days after my birthday in 2014, so I only missed the challenge by about 48 hours.

☐ 7) Start recycling

Plan: I'm amazed at how much trash we generate. Time to be smarter here and get the kids involved. I made some coin with cans in my youth!

Actual: I set up three bins in the garage for collecting plastic, cans, and newspaper. The kids were on the ball at first, and even helped a bit throughout the year. But Dad did most of the bagging and separating. Now there are ten or so bags in the garage waiting to be turned in. So we started and are still doing it, but I can't quite call it a win.

☒ 8) Have a family service project

Plan: This could get partially combined with the recycling efforts. I want us to pick a cause and do something to support it on a sustained basis instead of a one-time deal.

Actual: Total and utter failure. Call it busyness and lack of focus. It happens. But I still want to do this in the coming year. We are so blessed and I want my kids to see that and experience the joy of giving.

Note: Failed in 2014 as well. We do some giving, but the service aspect is what I was aiming for. It just hasn't been a big enough priority yet.

☑ 9) Visit a museum or attend a symphony/play/opera

Plan: A little culture for the uncultured.

Actual: Alice Cooper wasn't what I had in mind when

I wrote this goal, but it sure was a good show on November 1st! And it was Anna's first rock concert, so double-win that it wasn't some freaky screamo band, but a living legend and one of Heather's favorites. Dad wins this one!

☑ 10) Family Vacation

Plan: Normally this consists of visiting family, which is nice. But Disney's been on the short list for several years. Maybe we won't visit the mouse, but we need to do something and enjoy ourselves together.

Actual: Time and finances caught up with this one, so it turned into a big family trip to see family for Thanksgiving. But considering the distance and the great time we had, I say it counts! The mouse can wait a while.

☑ 11) Read the entire Bible

Plan: I've read all the way through the Bible twice since I became a Christian 10 years ago. But I've been inconsistent the last few years and need to sharpen my faith.

Actual: I was tracking my progress every month during my updates. I started strong, then hit the Psalms and slowed down. I think I read about 100 pages of my 1,339-page Bible in the last five days of the year, but I finished the Book of Revelation while fireworks lit up the neighborhood.

☒ 12) Twelve Dates with My Wife

Plan: As much as the weekend getaway is important, regular date nights are probably more important. The kids aren't quite old enough to leave at home alone yet, and this is something we've failed to do enough of.

Actual: Ten out of twelve isn't bad, especially considering our track record over the last few years. Still, I can't call this one a win and will need to put more effort into it for the future (which is already looking better!).

☑ 13) Visit Congress or AL Legislature

Plan: This is partly because I'm a political junkie with dreams (nightmares?) of the White House, but also because I'm actually involved in the legislative process now as a school board member in my hometown. I'm not Mr. Smith, but it's important to be involved in the process.

Actual: My January 2013 trip to Congress didn't work out, but on April 24th, I visited the Alabama Legislature and was recognized on the floor of the House. Very cool, and a big win!

Business and Personal Development

☑ 14) Publish my first book

Plan: I started my book in 2010, but it's been derailed a few times—mostly because I want it to be good enough to be proud of instead of just being something I popped out. This is the year! The last 10% is the hardest part, but that's all that's left.

Actual: It was the year, and probably the biggest single accomplishment of 2013. *Conquer the Entrepreneur's Kryptonite: Simple Strategic Planning for You and Your Business* was published on June 14th, has sold hundreds of copies with thousands given away, and is still getting rave reviews from readers.

☒ 15) Produce ten products (e-books, audio programs, etc.)

Plan: While the book may be the big one for the year, I also want to produce a lot more content.

Actual: It's hard to call this one a failure, but by the numbers, it is. Still, the book was published, the Kindle edition was published, and the audiobook was published. My coaching group program is almost complete (see below), and I have several e-books in the works. I feel good on this one, even with the red X.

☑ 16) Conduct group coaching course

Plan: I've taught a lot of people through the years, especially at Free Agent Academy. But I want group coaching to be a strong focus for the year, and a cornerstone of my business.

Actual: I started the Conquer 2014 coaching group on November 14th with twelve members. We had a lot of calls and messages, and those who stuck with it now have solid plans for their businesses in 2014. I'm so excited for them, and can't wait to share this program with the world in the coming days and weeks. It is going to help a lot of people!

☑ 17) Conduct first STRATOP

Plan: Last year I was certified in the most amazing strategic planning process I've ever seen. This year, I'm looking for businesses and organizations in need of a strategic plan. Marketing will be the key.

Actual: I had to make a substitution, but it was a great one! I spent two days with my friend and client Teri Miller in November. After 20-plus intense hours, we built a plan for her Mommy Sabbatical business for 2014 and beyond. She's on fire and I can't wait to see what she does! As for STRATOP, I still need to nail down my marketing approach, but it's a great program and I'm looking forward to doing more with it.

Note: Teri did do great things in 2014, hosting several events. I need to get a good STRATOP marketing plan.

☑ 18) Finish my office

Plan: There's a great shed in my backyard. It's got power and walls, but needs paint and flooring. Time to get it finished and move in!

Actual: Although I finished the office in May and was able to move in and work, there are still constant needs and desires in here (I'm in it right now). But I have a sanctuary of my own where I can work in peace and quiet. Total win!

☐ 19) Establish LLC

Plan: In order to take my business to the next level, I need to make it more official. But this will require the proper revenue to make it worthwhile. So is this really a revenue goal?

Actual: While this was my plan, I actually punted on it. Working as a Sole Proprietor is still the best structure for what I'm doing, and there were no real advantages to creating an LLC yet, so I didn't do it. One day, and hopefully sooner rather than later, that will change. Because it was the right thing to do, I'll call it a draw instead of a failure.

☑ 20) Start a podcast

Plan: Similar to the products goal above, it's important to get my voice out there. People have to get to know me to understand the value I have to offer. This will go a long way in doing that.

Actual: The *Conquer Your Kryptonite* podcast isn't live yet, but pre-production meetings have been going on for the last month or so. My producer is Bret Farmer, and we even recorded a first show but decided to tweak the format before doing additional recordings.

Hopefully the first episode will launch this month. Since the goal says "start," I call it a win!

Note: The podcast didn't launch until October, as 2014 was a bit crazy on the home front. But Bret is still producing the show, which is co-hosted by my friend Megan Burns. Check it out at ConquerYourKryptonite.com/podcast.

☒ 21) Consistently wake up between 5 and 6 am

Plan: My friend Andy Traub just launched a great book called *Early to Rise*. I'm a night owl, but this will be a positive transformation if I can pull it off!

Actual: I'm still a night owl. Total fail. And I'm okay with that for now.

Note: Still a night owl....

☑ 22) Teach a community class (other than FPU)

Plan: I'm getting ready to start my 17th FPU class—it's time to do something new. And there are so many ideas in my head.

Actual: It wasn't what I intended to do, but the opportunity I had to speak at a local organization on October 18th will have to serve as a substitution here. I am lining up my own courses soon, but this went so well and was so well-received, I say it counts.

☐ 23) Join/Start Local Mastermind/Networking Group

Plan: I have incredible connections all over the Internet, but surprisingly few locally. It's a weakness created from being an introverted road warrior who has spent more than half of the last 10 years traveling. I have one strong possibility with a local friend to be named later. If that doesn't work out, I start my own!

Actual: Discussions with my friend never materialized, but I did have an awesome weekend in Charlotte masterminding and coaching with my friends Steve and Jody Berkey and Mark Burch. I still want to do a local group on a regular basis, but the quality of the time and continuing connection from this meet up allows me to call the goal a draw.

Note: Local is still difficult, but in January of 2014, I joined an incredible Mastermind program led by Dan Miller of 48Days.com. It has profoundly affected my life and business.

☒ 24) Make 100 blog posts

Plan: I have to be producing on the blog, and the posts have to be more than what they have been. Starting now.

Actual: This update post made it a total of forty for the year. Sad, but maybe blogging regularly just isn't my thing. I like to write when an idea hits me, then share it with the world right away. That's not realistic, though, and if I'm going to go pro I need to be a pro. Schedules, themes, and building a bank of articles is on the table for the future. Blogs need to have a consistency about them to be successful. Fail, but I learned lessons in the attempt (and I wrote some really good stuff when I did post!).

Note: I probably did worse in 2014 and am re-examining my entire writing strategy as soon as this book is published.

Fitness and Adventure

☑ 25) Ride a Century (100-mile single bike event)

Plan: Last year I participated in two organized bike rides. One was forty-five miles and the other was thirty miles. My eyes are set on the Juvenile Diabetes Research Foundation (JDRF) Nashville Ride this September for my first century. But with some other rides in mind (Bike MS North Alabama, Hotter'N Hell 100, Hot 100) and lots of practice, I may do it more than once!

Actual: It was quite a feeling raising my bike over my head in Nashville on September 21st. I completed 103 miles in the JDRF Ride for a Cure and raised more than $2,000. Wow!

☑ 26) Complete first 5K race

Plan: I don't like running. But it's probably good for me. And the Gator Fest 5K supports my school system, so I'll be sweating it out on March 9th.

Actual: Totally killed this one with a personal record for a 5K of 33:36. I'm not fast, but I did it!

☒ 27) Drive a race car

Plan: Thanks to LivingSocial, this one is bought and paid for. And I get to do it with my wife (I mean she gets to drive a race car, also).

Actual: I sadly have to take an incomplete on this one,

though it wasn't for lack of trying. The date I planned for March was cancelled, and then the rescheduled date in December was rained out. Still hoping to jump behind the wheel in February, the next window of opportunity.

☑ 28) Complete second Spartan race

Plan: November is a long way from now. But after last year, I better start training now!

Actual: Spartan races are hard and this one was no exception. I was in better shape than I was for the first one, but not enough to record any amazing times. But then again, I don't cheat—I do all of the penalty burpees. Mission complete!

☑ 29) Attend a NASCAR event

Plan: I haven't been to a race in a long time. Talladega, Daytona, Bristol?

Actual: The Charlotte Mastermind meeting just happened to be scheduled at the same time the NASCAR guys and gals were in town, and my buddy Mark Burch just happened to have a friend who got us suite tickets and pit passes for the Nationwide race. It wasn't the Cup series, but it was classy!

☒ 30) Take a firearms safety class

Plan: The police department in my hometown has occasional classes where we learn about firearms laws and safety, then head to the firing range. Sounds like a great date!

Actual: Again, multiple missed opportunities due to scheduling conflicts. I hope they continue to offer the classes because I will be there!

☒ 31) BMI of 25 or lower

Plan: Okay, BMI may not be the best fitness indicator, but I'm right on the line, so it's a good target. And with all this exercise, I'm bound to lose 10 pounds and get there, right?

Actual: I came unbelievably close on this one—within two pounds. I'm in the best shape I've been in a long time. But I didn't make it. P90X3 and a better diet start next week...got to get in shape for some more crazy adventures in 2014!

Note: I completed a month or so of P90X3 before I had to quit due to some family issues. But I hit my BMI goal a few months later (for one day). Time to put the Tony Horton DVDs back in!

☑ 32) Complete a fast

Plan: I want to go fast, so I have the bike and racecar. Doing a fast? It's something new and should be interesting. More research needed.

Actual: I gave up all soda and pop and soda pop and Coke (depending on where you live) for forty days from Mardi Gras to Easter. I didn't continue to fast, but I did it when it counted.

❎ 33) Record two million steps in 2013

Plan: They say 10,000 steps a day are needed to be healthy. That equates to 3,650,000 steps in 2013, which is not going to happen, as I sit at a computer all day. But I can do better than my poor average of 2,000 to 3,000 steps per day. Doubling that seems like a worthy step in the right direction.

Actual: This was a moral victory, but a failure nonetheless. My 2013 total from January 1st to December 31st was only 1,934,749. I needed another 65,251 steps, or a measly 179 more per day. Failing to do my daily tracking after the half marathon got me.

Note: The power of tracking to a goal was highlighted with this one in 2014. Not tracking numbers and not having racing goals reduced my level of activity by about 30%.

☑ 34) Complete the Manitou Springs Incline

Plan: It's been slightly illegal for years (soon to be legal), but definitely a fitness challenge for the hundreds who do it every day. My next trip to Colorado has to include time for the incline!

Actual: I made it to Colorado and saw the Incline, but scheduling didn't allow me to make an attempt. So I substituted some good mountain hikes instead, one with the Miller family and one on my own for a bit of prayer and quiet time with God. Win.

☒ 35) Ride over 1,200 miles

Plan: Those big rides are going to require some serious training. There's nothing like putting a number down to serve as a target. I should blow this away if I hit my rides.

Actual: It was a nice number: 1,200—just 100 miles per month. I fell short a bit, totaling only 898. The winter got cold and I just stopped going out. No excuses. It was still an amazing year on my bike and I'm looking forward to setting new personal records in 2014.

Note: Turns out 2014 was a bad year for biking. I did two events, and barely rode with everything going on. I simply didn't make it a priority, so it didn't happen.

☑ 36) Wildcard #1: Attempt a Half Marathon

Plan: I added this one at the encouragement of Steve and Jody Berkey. The key word is "attempt."

Actual: Yet with training and perseverance, I did it! I ran the Marine Corps Half Marathon in Fredericksburg, VA, on May 19th. And I think I'll do another one someday, when my toenails grow back.

Note: It took a year for my toenails to return to normal. I'll need new shoes if I ever try it again. I ran a single 5K in 2014.

☒ 37) Wildcard #2: Send a Letter to My Address in England

Plan: While searching Google Maps, I found a house

in England with the same number and street name as ours in Alabama (our street name uses British spelling for some reason, making it a bit odd). The plan is to send a letter or package to them.

Actual: It simply never happened. I thought about it a few times, especially as Christmas rolled around. But we never did it.

❎ 38) Wildcard #3: Make My Military Shadowbox

Plan: I have never displayed my military gear, and I want to have something so my kids understand military service better. I grew up in it, but they have never seen me in uniform except in pictures.

Actual: I have the frame and found a bunch of my old things, but never got the project going. I will, but can't call this one complete.

☑ 39) Wildcard #4: Play Lasertag

Plan: I never defined this one through the year, so I'm thinking back to a birthday party we went to at a bowling alley.

Actual: And at that party I finally played laser tag. I always wanted to as a kid, but never did. I'm not sure why, because it was a lot of fun and a great workout. I'm cheating a bit by claiming it now, but why not? It was a blast!

⊠ 40) Wildcard #5

Plan: Never defined.

Actual: Goals that are never defined cannot be accomplished. I left room for wildcards, but should have set deadlines to nail them down. Lesson learned.

Final Thoughts

That's a record of 22-14-4. A winning record, but I factor in a few other things to call this a successful experiment and a great year:

I didn't take it easy. These were ambitious goals that required extensive effort.

My failures were rarely complete-and-utter failures (and most were a result of not even attempting them). I came close and I did amazing things, even when I came up short of the goal.

Bottom line: I had an awesome year! I hope you attempt something similar and experience the joy I have over the course of the last twelve months.

ACKNOWLEDGEMENTS

The Story of This Book

Having already written and published one book (and having started publishing for others), I knew the work involved in getting this one written, polished, edited, formatted, printed, sold, and shipped. It is not an easy process, especially when you do most of it yourself.

Yet it wasn't just me doing it.

My wife didn't object to my crazy forty goals, though she probably rolled her eyes a bit when I first came up with the idea (no doubt thinking I would force her to join in).

My friends embraced the idea and let me run with it, cheering me every step of the way. Jody and Steve Berkey were the most consistent and the loudest. I cherish their friendship. We have a pact that the first ones to make a million dollars will take the others to Hawaii. Now I just need to sell 300,000+ copies and book the trip for us.

I had other friends start their own challenges based on my experiment. That was an honor and further encouragement that I was doing something worthwhile. Thank you, Amber Hendrickson, Toni Amequito, and Melinda McAndrews. (If I missed anyone else, I either didn't know or simply forgot.)

I'm not positive, but I believe it was Jared Easley who first encouraged me to turn this adventure into a book. He was interviewing me about 40 Before 40 on his podcast, *Starve the Doubts* (with co-host Jody Maberry). Both Jared and Jody have encouraged me many times since, and it eventually stuck.

The book idea stayed buried in my mind for many months—difficult months of kids in the hospital, my grandmother's bypass surgery and recovery, the loss of my job, and my struggle to either find a new job or get my business going. (The year 2014 probably deserves a book of its own, but I'm not sure the last chapter has been written.)

I was driving to North Alabama for a school board convention one day in December 2014 when the title *Challenge Accepted!* hit me.

My daughter and I had started (and finished) every episode of *How I Met Your Mother* on Netflix, where the phrase is a favorite of character Barney Stinson played by Neil Patrick Harris. Maybe all those hours staring at a screen paid off!

With the title in place and the ChallengeAccepted.info URL secured that evening, I knew I had to write this book. I had to accept this challenge!

Megan Burns and I co-host the *Conquer Your*

Kryptonite Show podcast, which launched in October of 2014 (starting a podcast was one of the original 40 Before 40 goals). Coming up with solid content is a struggle, but this story needed to be told and it would help me kick-start the book. So I outlined four episodes for January 2015 and they eventually became the four chapters of this book.

We started recording those episodes in late December, and at some point I promised to complete the book by the end of January. I did . . . kind of.

On the weekend before my deadline, with my family at the beach, I sat down to write my book as promised. Five days later, the first draft was complete and our audience could download it. [That means I essentially wrote this book in five days, not counting the two years of life lived to fill it.]

Special thanks to those who took the time to read it and provide input that made it better: Jason Vandehey, Ann Musico, Philip Havens, Celeste Davis, Tommy Blakeney and everyone in the Conquer Your Kryptonite Facebook group.

I planned to print it in February, but based on the feedback I was getting and the promotional ideas I was learning from Kimanzi Constable and Jimmy Burgess, I realized this was more than just a fun little project. This book could be more. So I delayed the printing date until May of 2015.

That time allowed new obstacles to develop, new fears to press in, and, predictably, procrastination to take root. There were times when I could have rushed it just to be finished, but I'm glad I've given myself time to explore its potential.

I'm also thankful to my editor, Jennifer Harshman of HarshmanServices.com. While I like to think I write good, she makes sure I write well.

This book has been my biggest intentional challenge of the year (unintentional challenges—aka regular life—have dominated so far).

Once the hoopla of the launch and some of those regular life challenges calm down a bit, I'll be launching into a new challenge myself. I'm going to need it to get back in shape, stay connected with my family, and keep living an intentional, purposeful life.

I hope you will start a challenge, too! Send me a note and let me know about it. Take a picture with your book and share it online (tag me!). I'll be cheering for you.

— James Woosley
james@woosleycoaching.com

ABOUT THE AUTHOR

James Woosley is an underachiever—only because he's constantly expanding his potential by doing something amazing, then immediately striving for more—knowing that his mind, body, and spirit have been stretched to a new level of possibilities.

As a business coach, consultant, and project manager, James helps people and organizations move ideas from the dreaming and planning stages to full implementation. He sets goals, plans strategically, and makes things happen—for himself and those around him.

In addition to *Challenge Accepted!*, he is the author of *Conquer the Entrepreneur's Kryptonite: Simple Strategic Planning for You and Your Business.*

Beyond serving his clients as a coach and consultant, writing books, participating as a newcomer to athletic events (Spartan Races, charity bicycle rides, running for no good reason), sitting on the board of education in his hometown and on the board of directors for the state school board association, James is a dedicated husband to his high school sweetheart, Heather, and a doting father to his children, Anna and Ian.

Learn more at WoosleyCoaching.com.

The Book that Started it All...

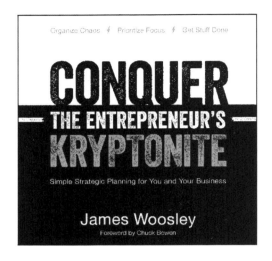

What is it that you want to achieve? Whatever it is, it's not going to be easy. Not if it's something BIG worth doing right.

But it can be made easier, and in doing so, make it look like it was easy to anyone who didn't see the blood and sweat you poured into your idea. Let's get to work!

Order online at ConquerYourKryptoite.com/resources or at Amazon, Audible, or iTunes.

The Conquer Your Kryptonite Show

Join hosts James Woosley and Megan Burns (The Naptime CEO) as they explore various "Kryptonites" faced by small business owners and entrepreneurs and discussing how to conquer them in a fun and informative half-hour show.

Featuring a Why-What-How format with clear Action Steps, this show will help you do business better.

Listen online at ConquerYourKryptonite.com/podcast. Also available on iTunes, iHeartRadio, TuneIn, Stitcher, Spreaker, SoundCloud, and more!

NOTES AND CHALLENGE IDEAS

Use the following pages to capture your thoughts and ideas as you read through or contemplate the book. The first step to making something real is to write it down. Have fun!

_____

_____

_____

_____

_____

_____

_____

_____

_____

_____

_____

_____

_____

_____

_____

_____

_____

_____

_____

NOTES AND CHALLENGE IDEAS

NOTES AND CHALLENGE IDEAS

_____

_____

_____

_____

_____

_____

_____

_____

_____

_____

_____

_____

_____

_____

_____

_____

_____

_____

_____

_____

_____

_____

_____

_____

NOTES AND CHALLENGE IDEAS

NOTES AND CHALLENGE IDEAS

NOTES AND CHALLENGE IDEAS

NOTES AND CHALLENGE IDEAS

_____

_____

_____

_____

_____

_____

_____

_____

_____

_____

_____

_____

_____

_____

_____

_____

_____

_____

_____

_____

_____

_____

_____

_____

_____

ChallengeAccepted.info

42001254R00088

Made in the USA
Charleston, SC
18 May 2015